M‚llwagen
Malbuch

Coloring Pages for Kids

Coloring Pages for Kids
An imprint of Ciparum LLC

M‚llwagen Malbuch
© 2017 Ciparum LLC
All rights reserved.
ISBN-10: 1-63589-500-6
ISBN-13:978-1-63589-500-1

Coloring Pages for Kids

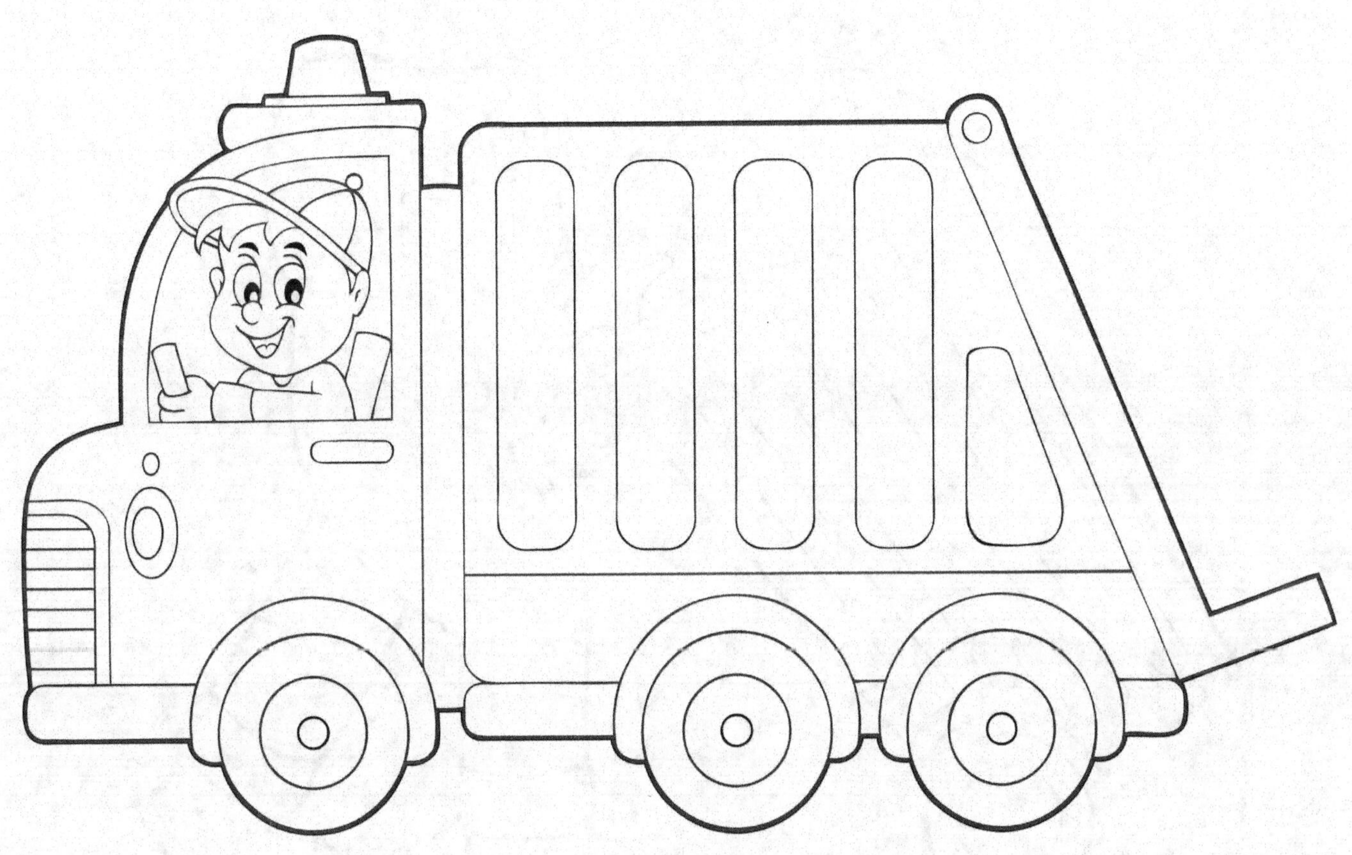

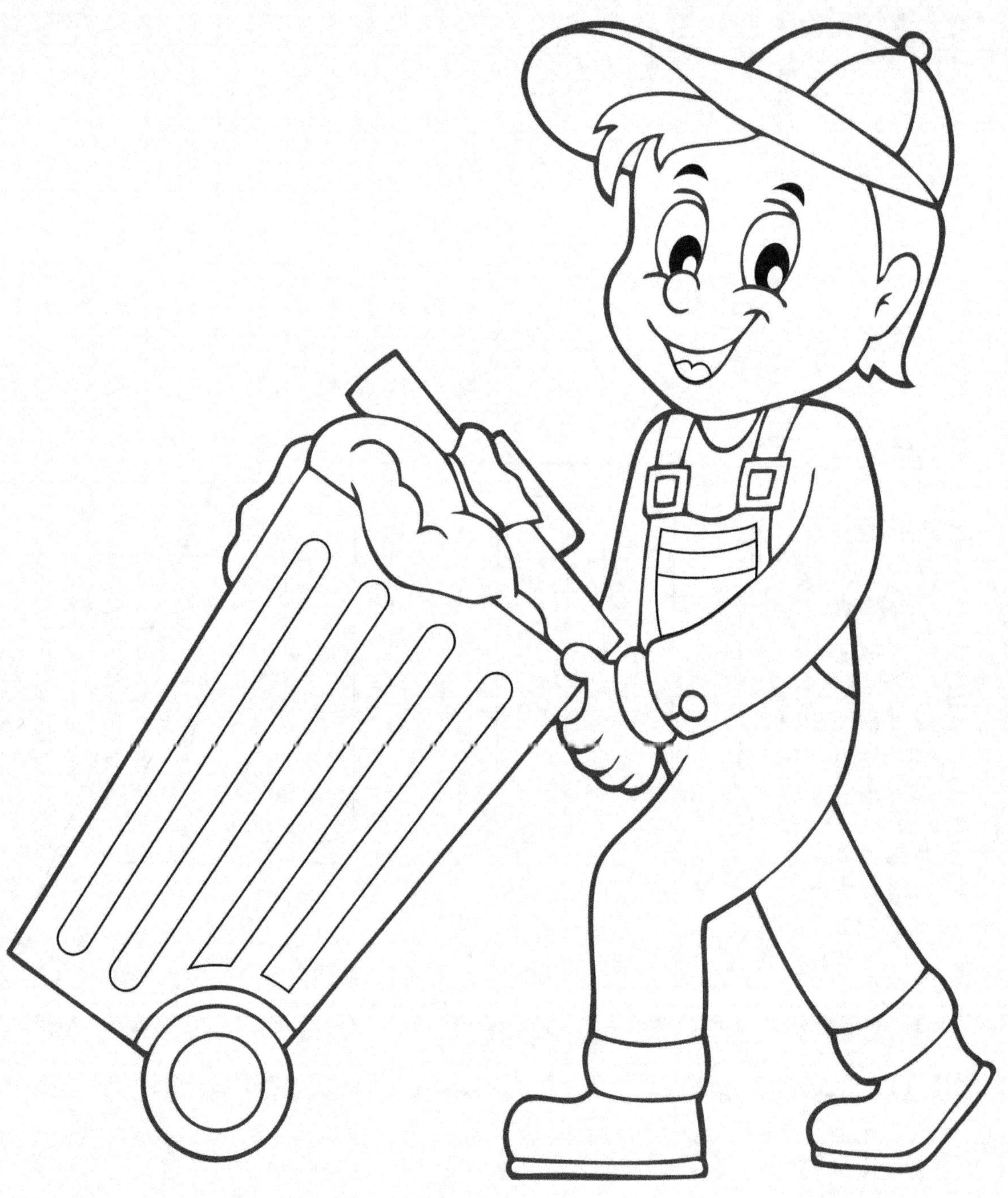

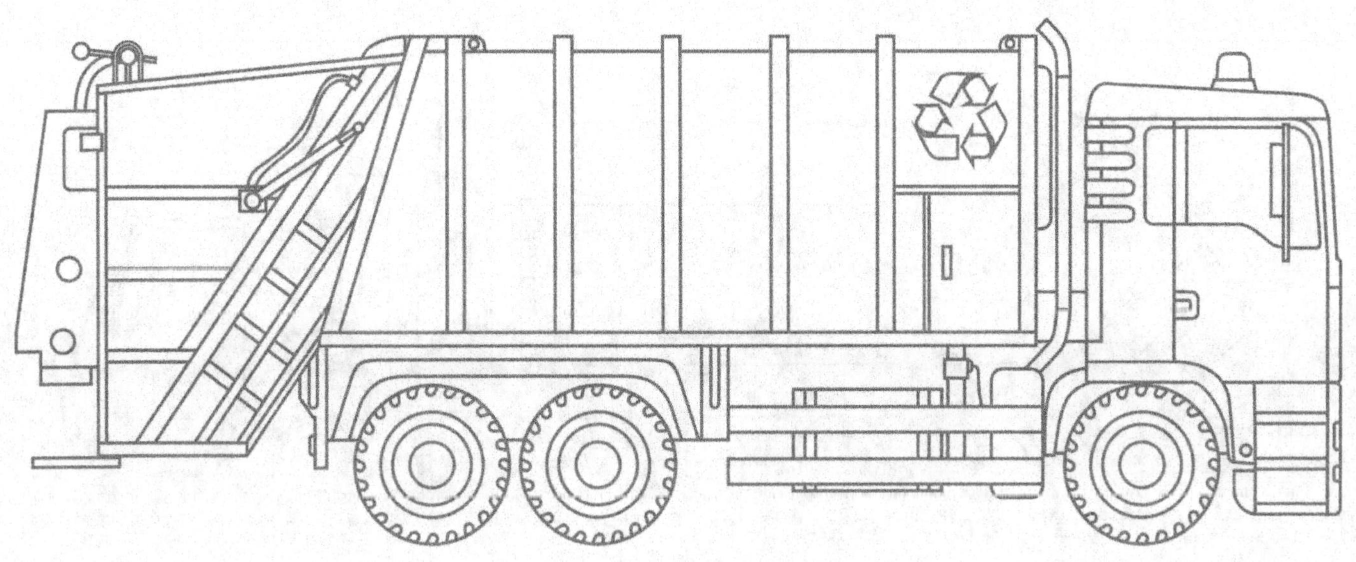

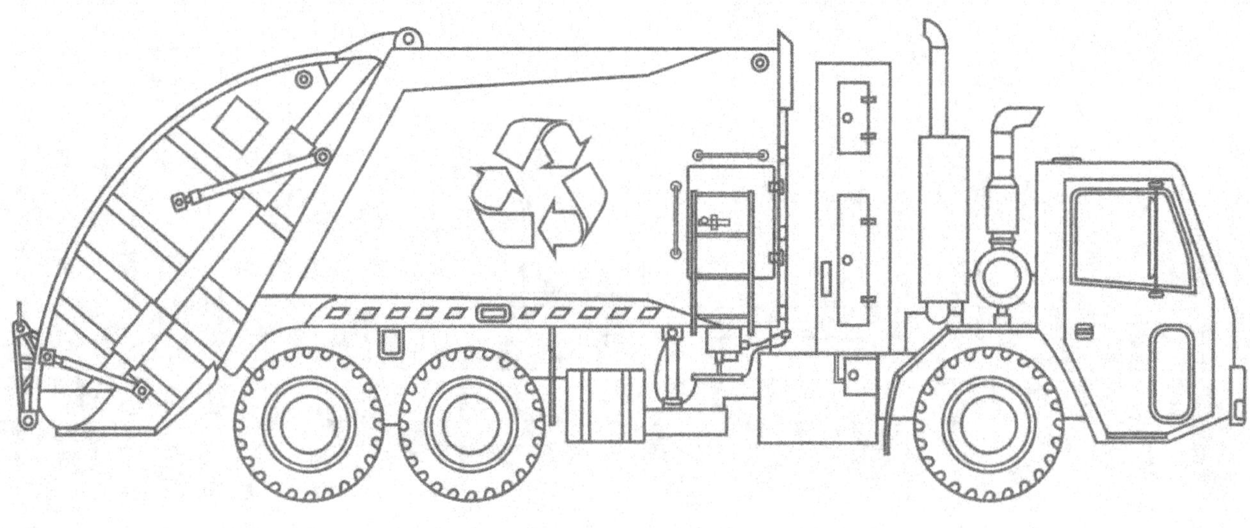

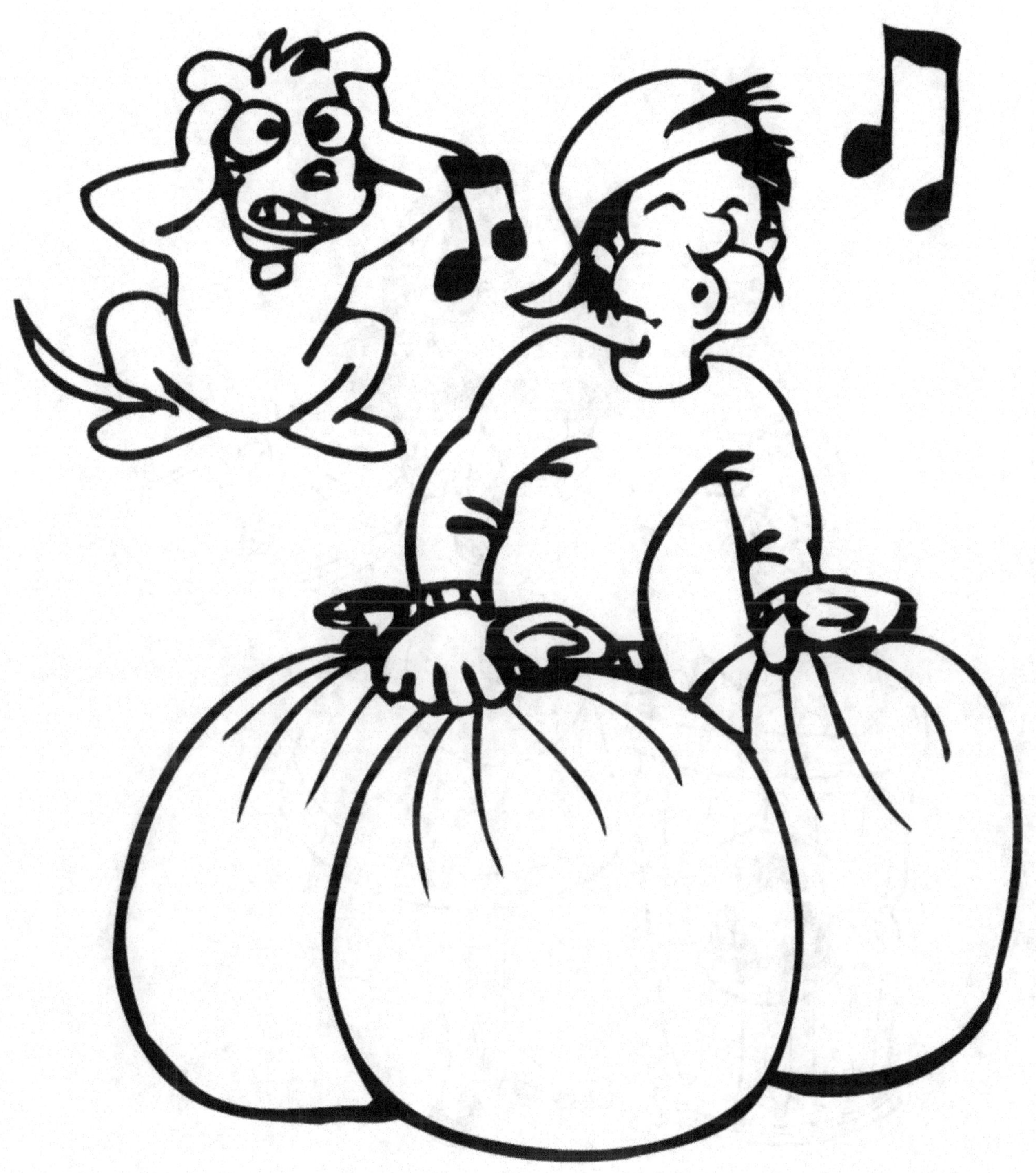

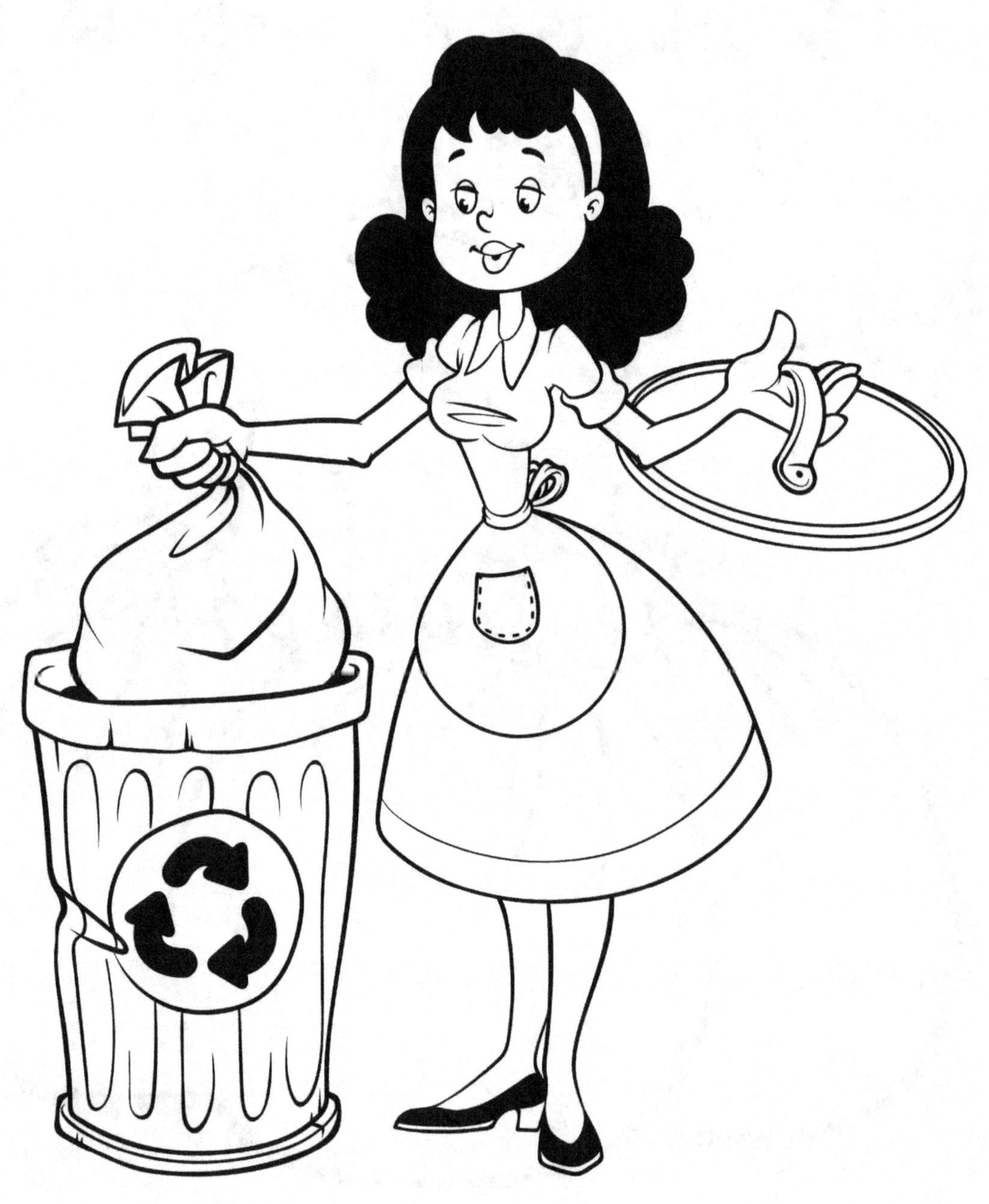

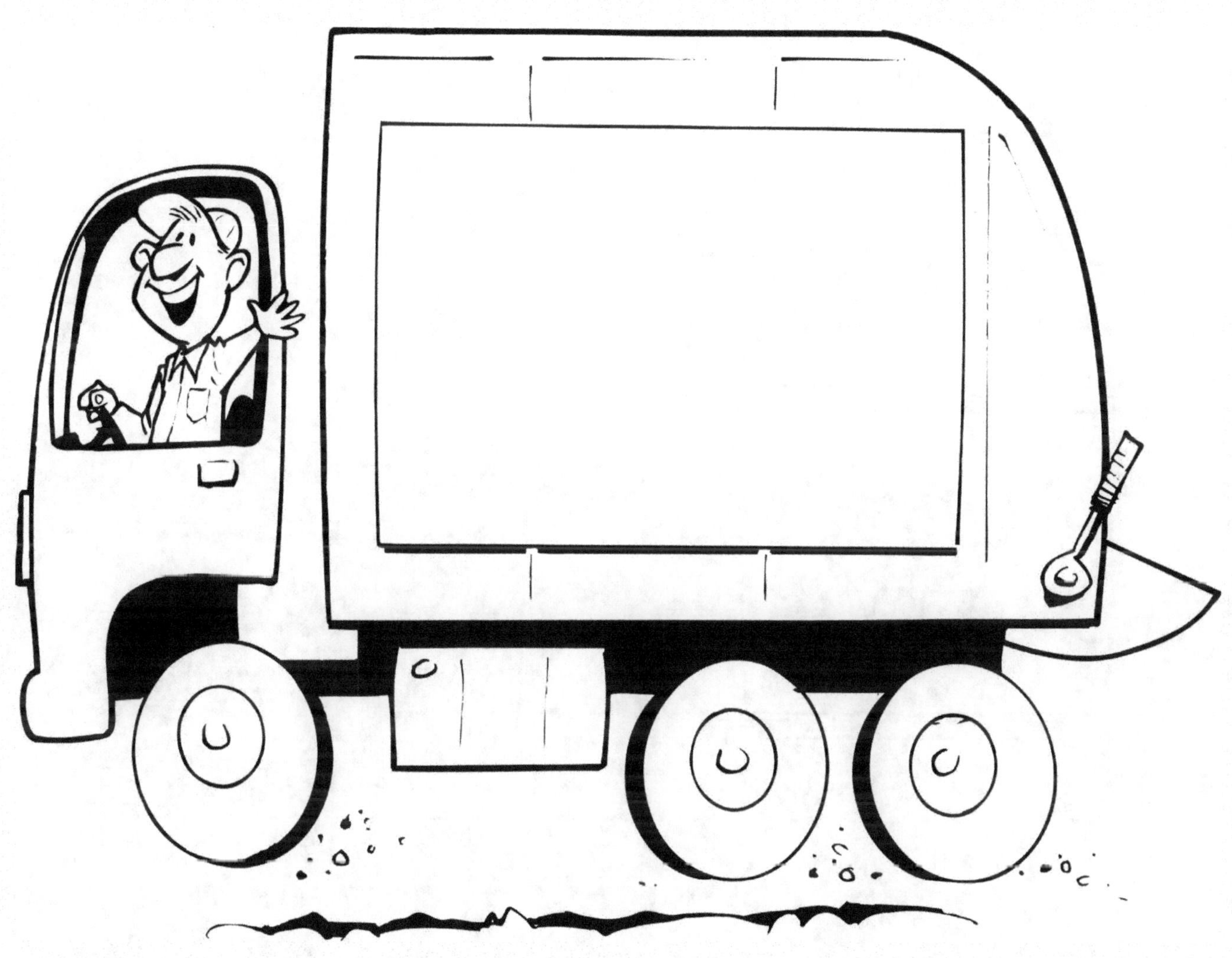

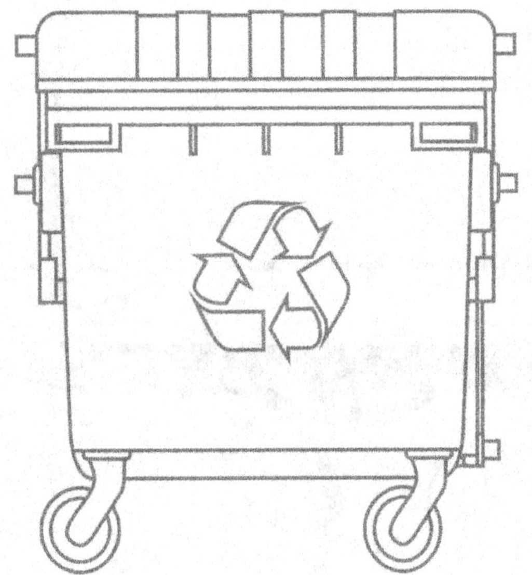 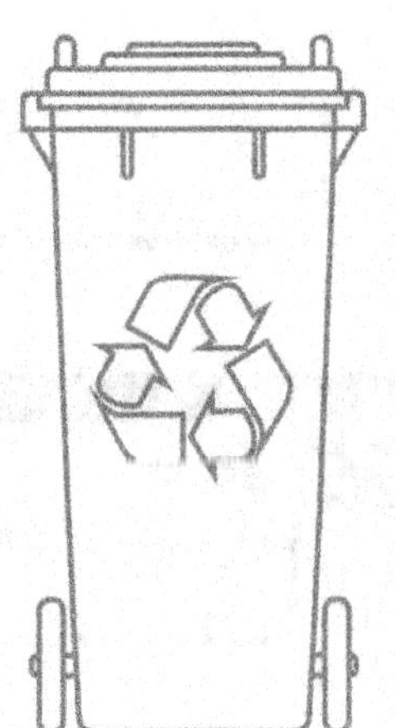 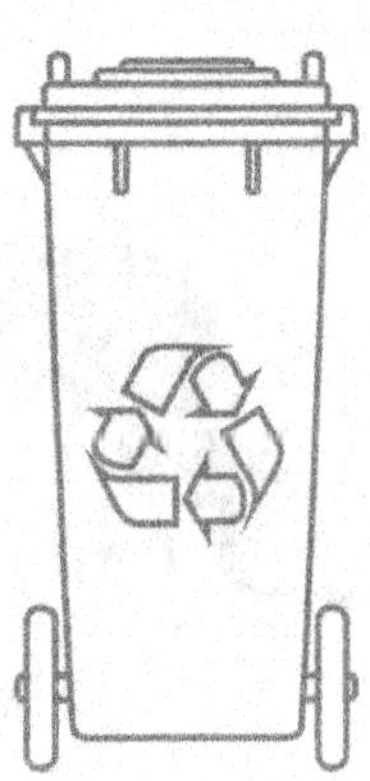

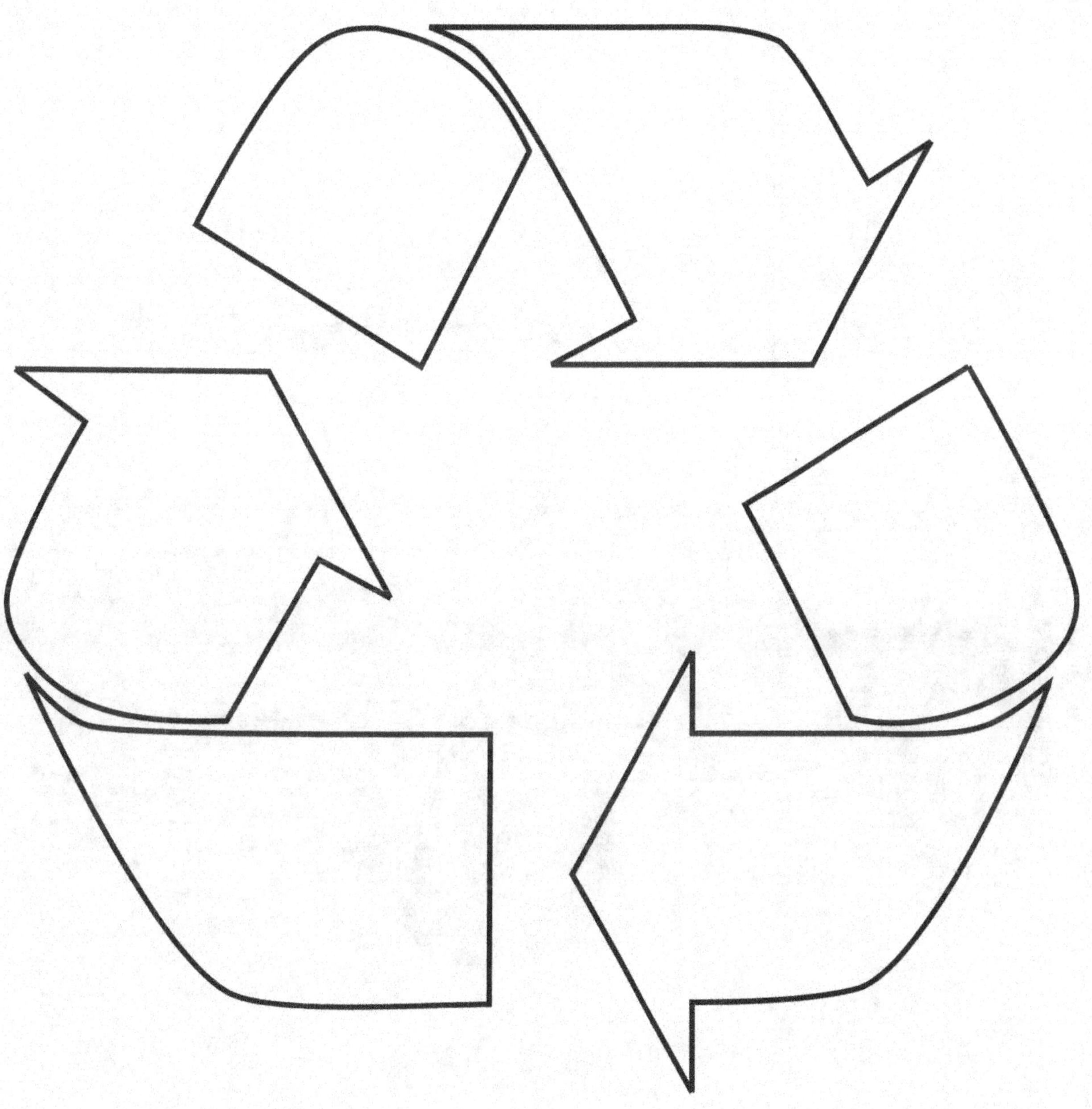

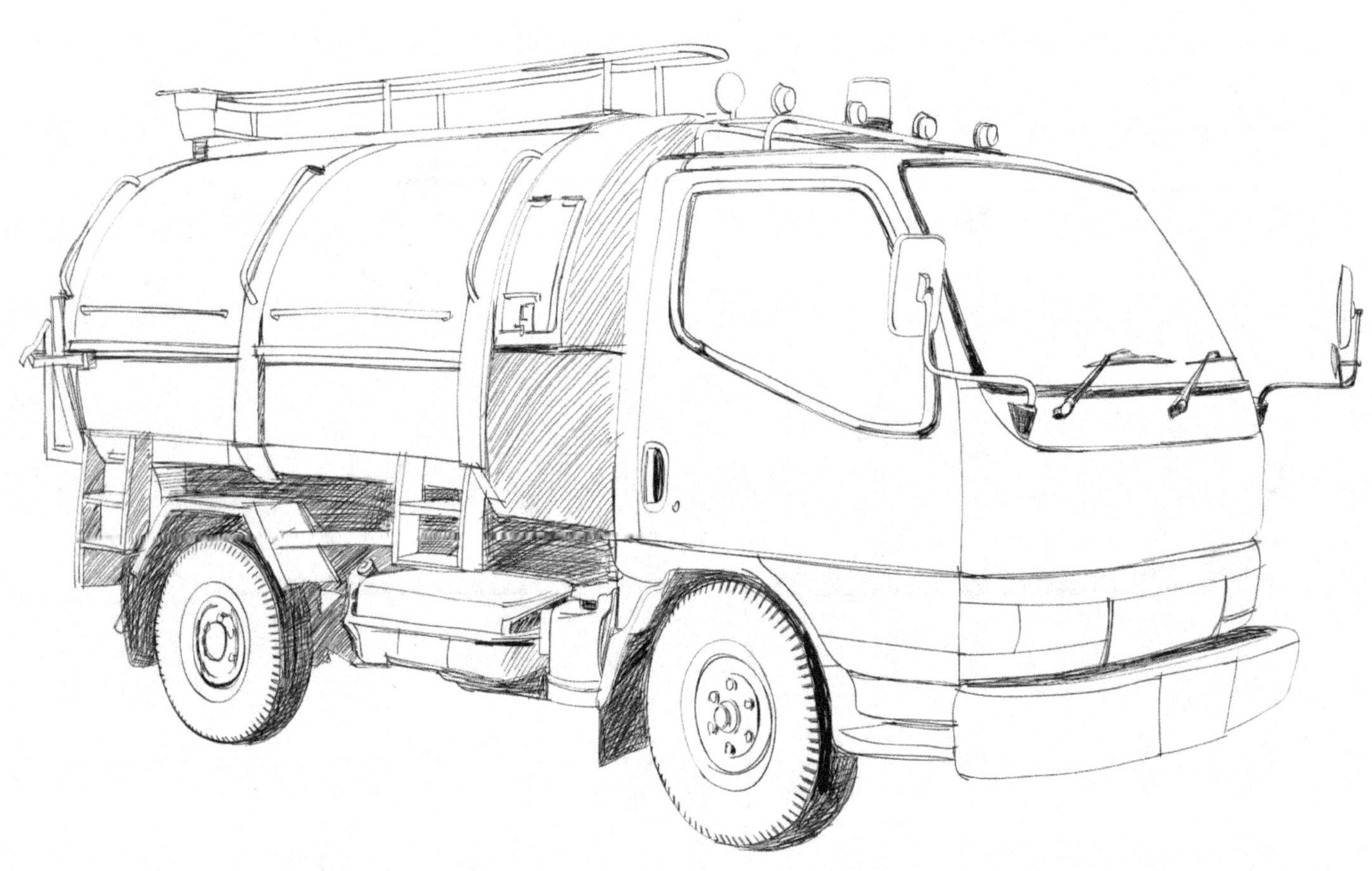

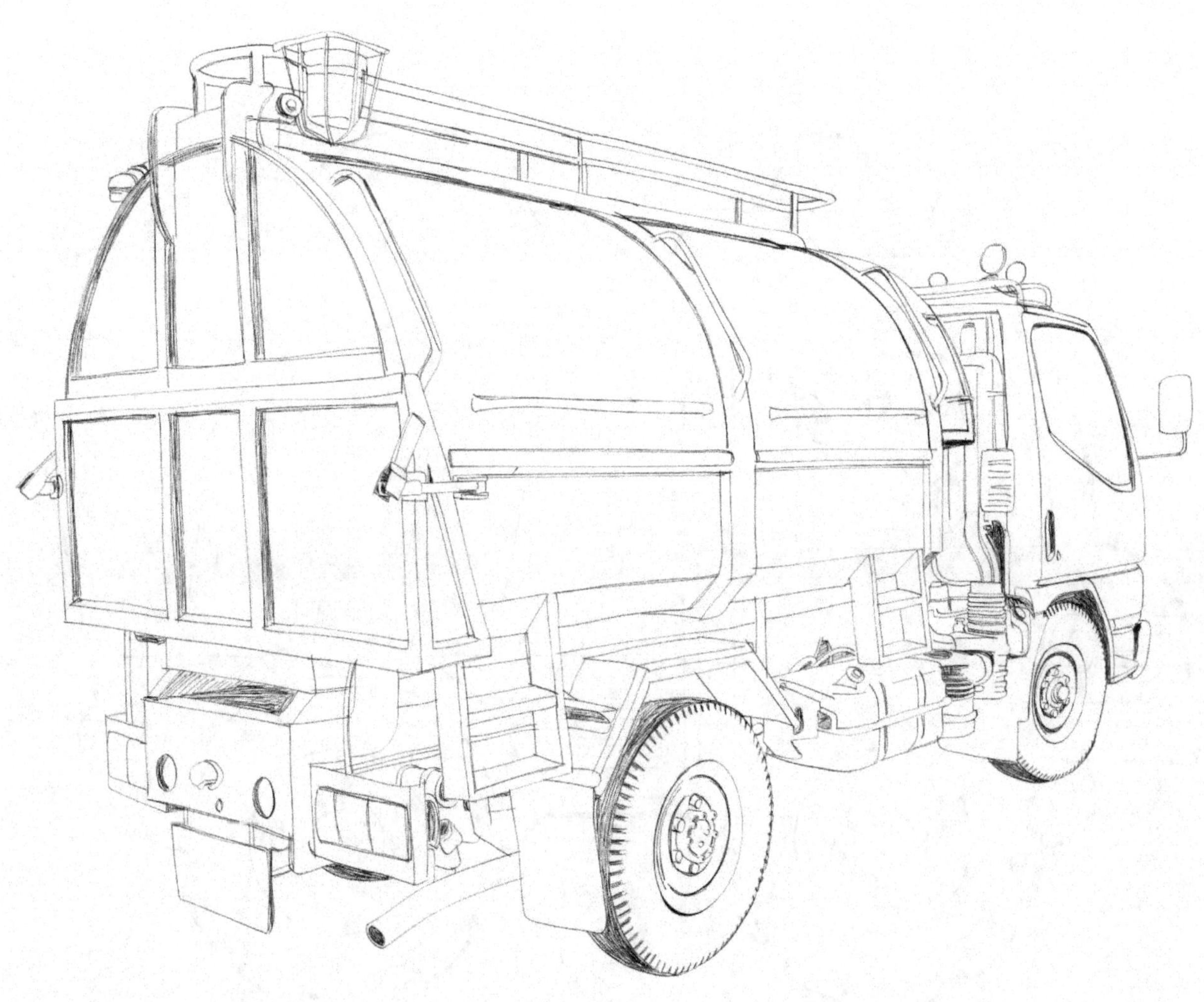

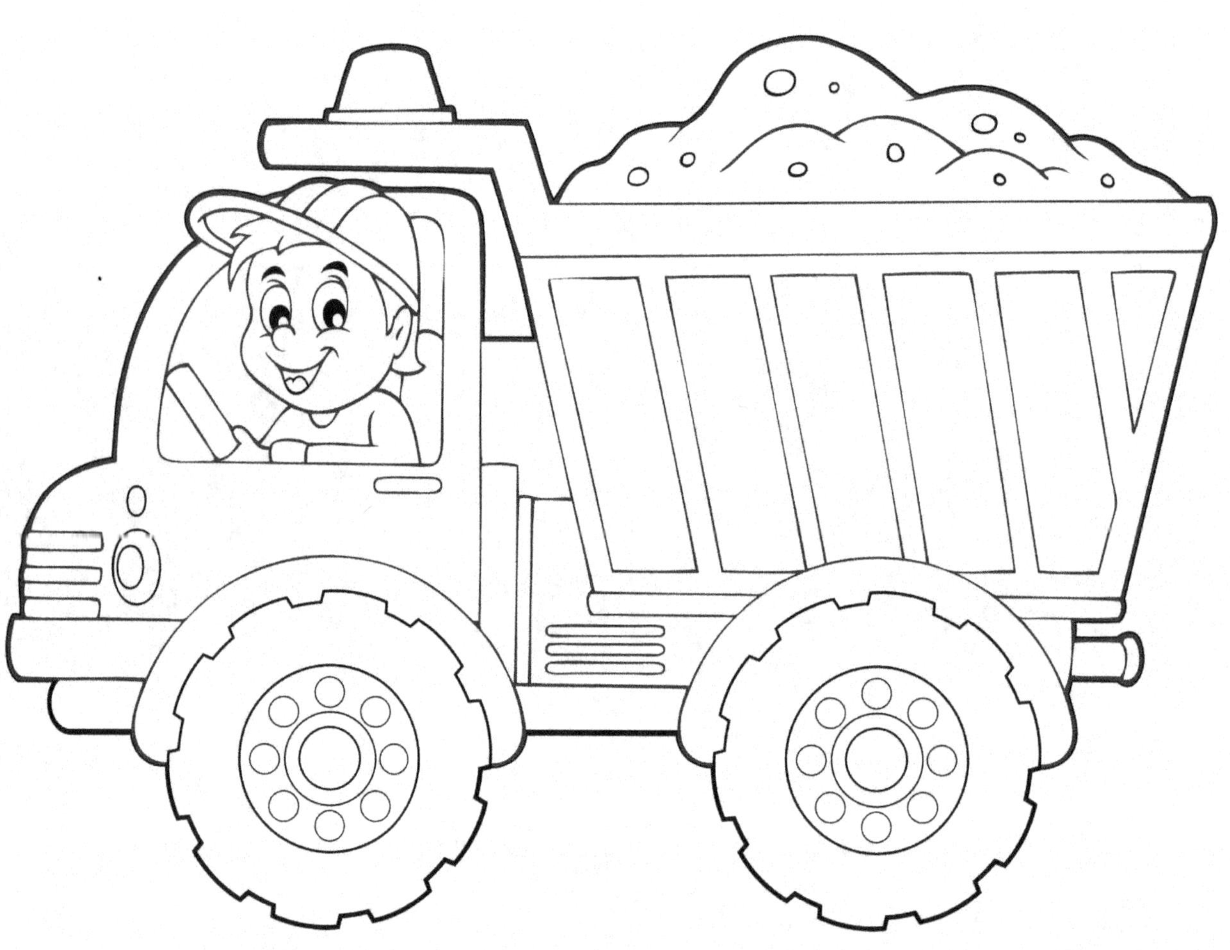

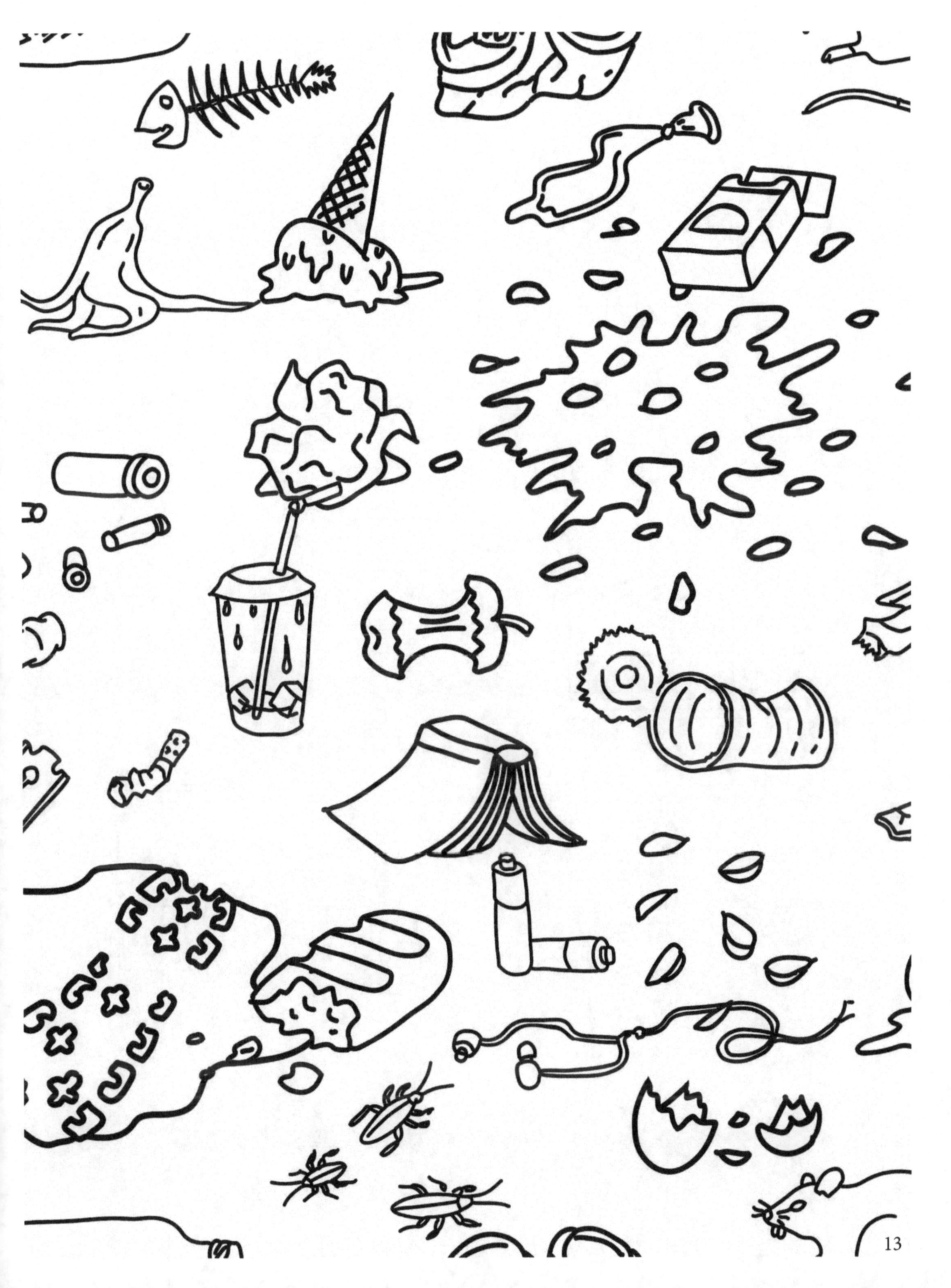

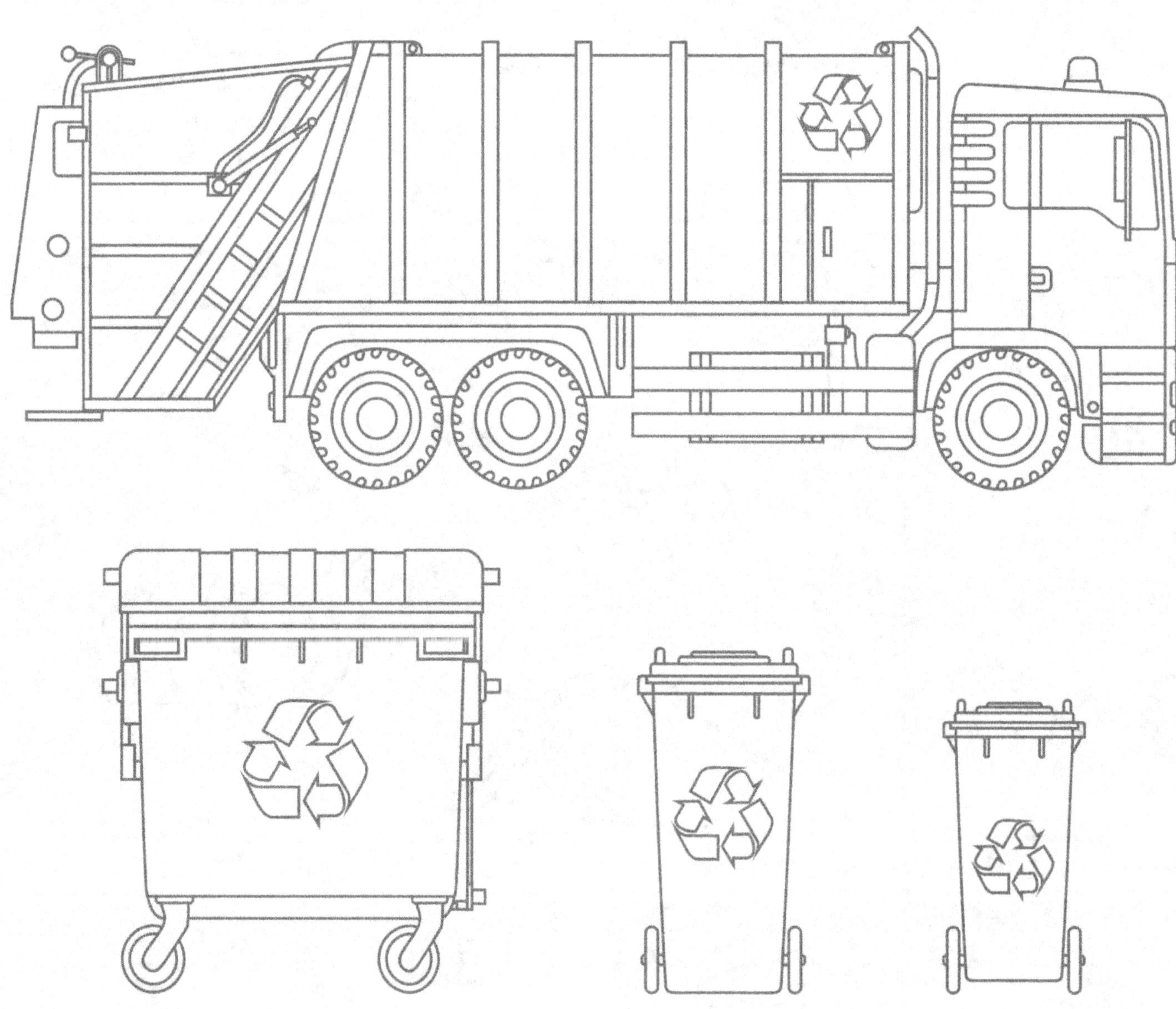

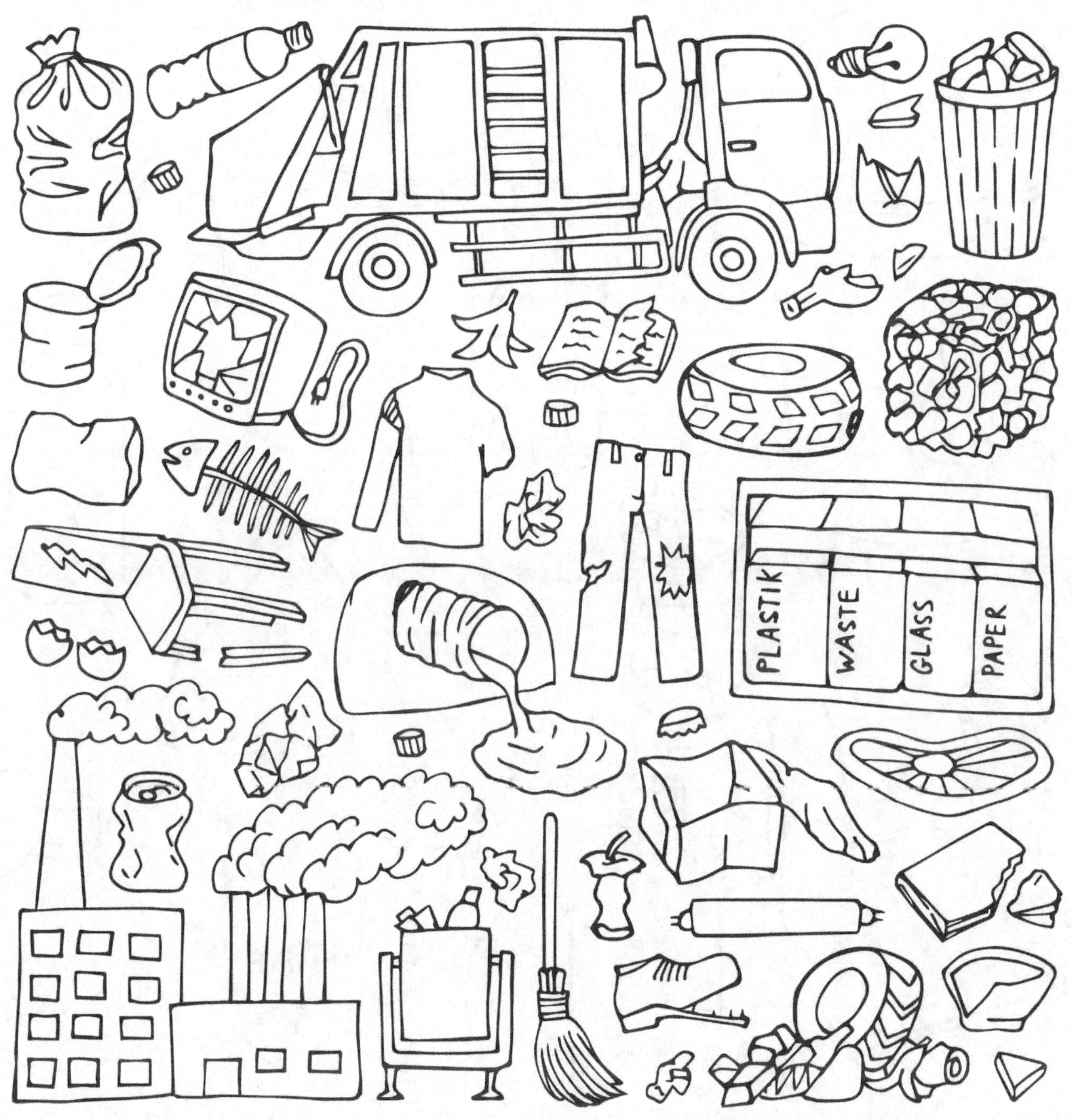

PLASTIK
WASTE
GLASS
PAPER

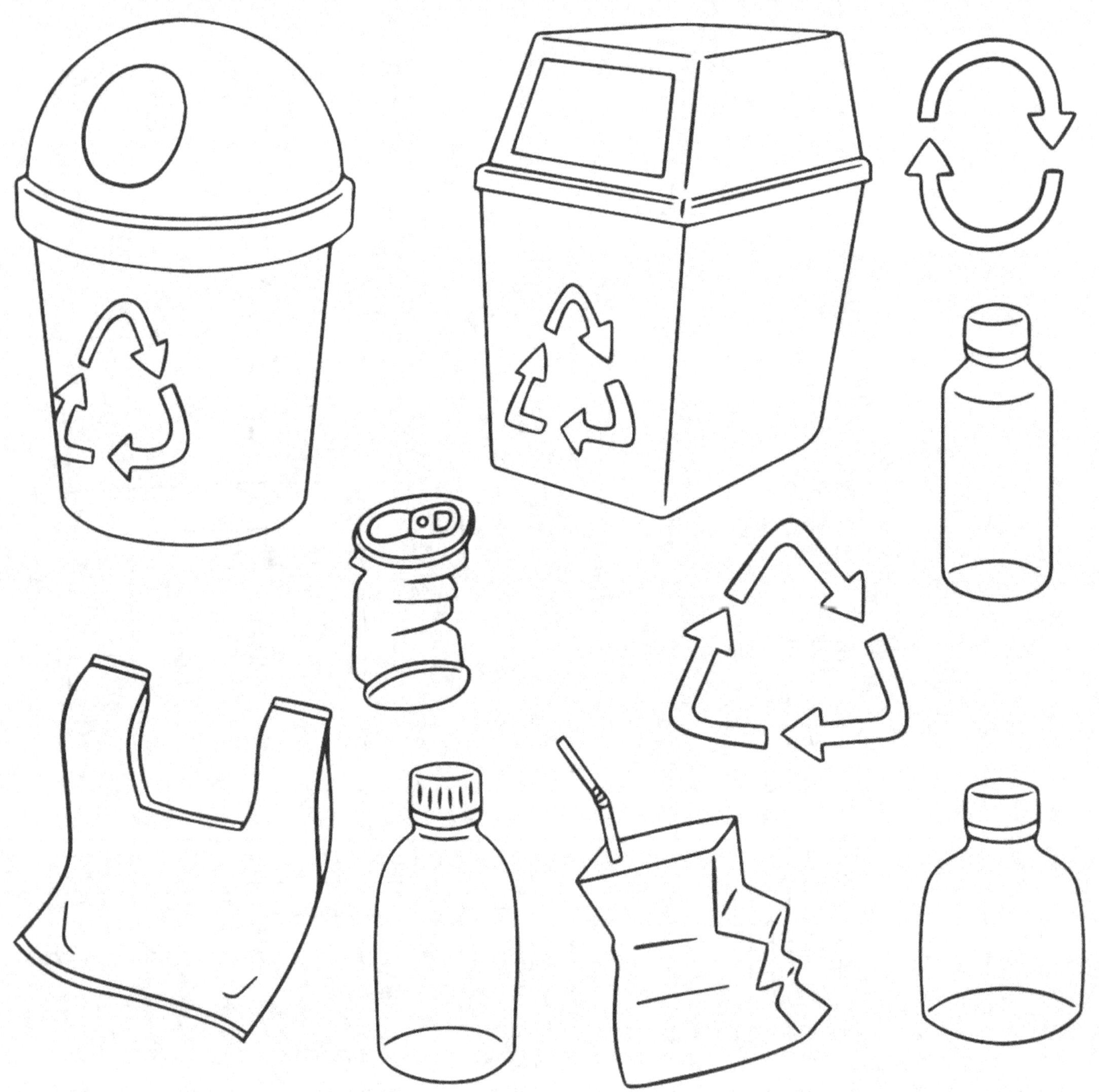

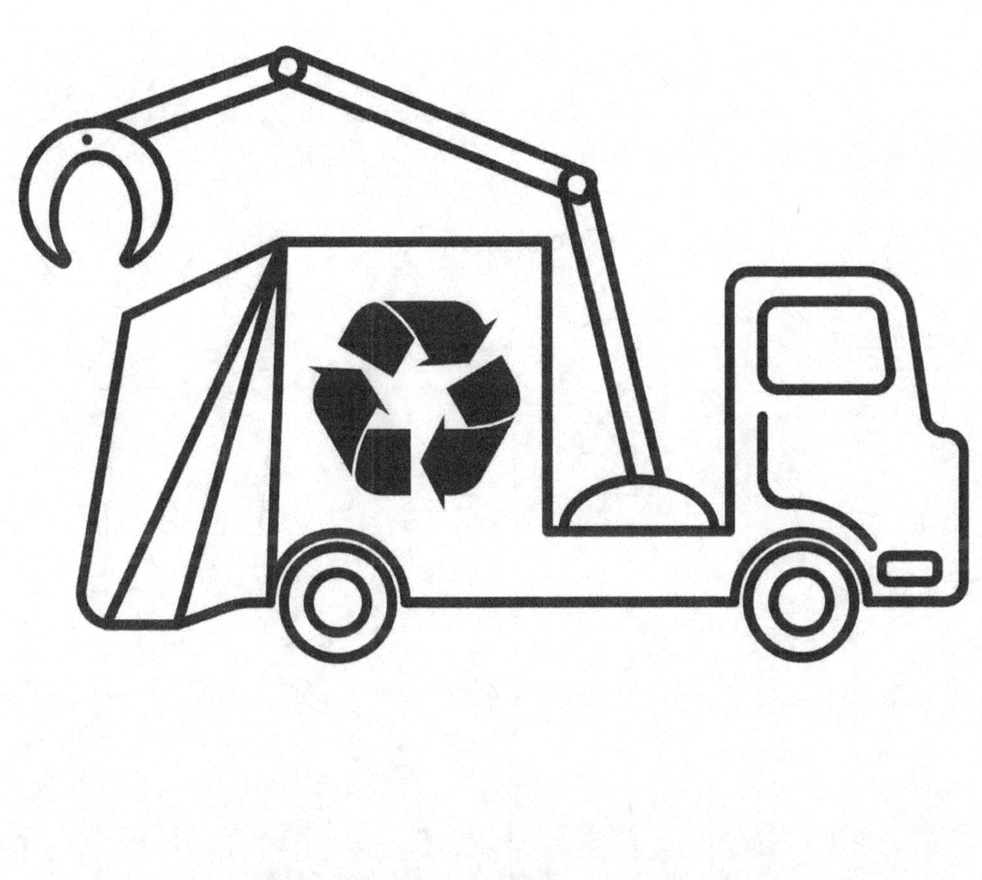
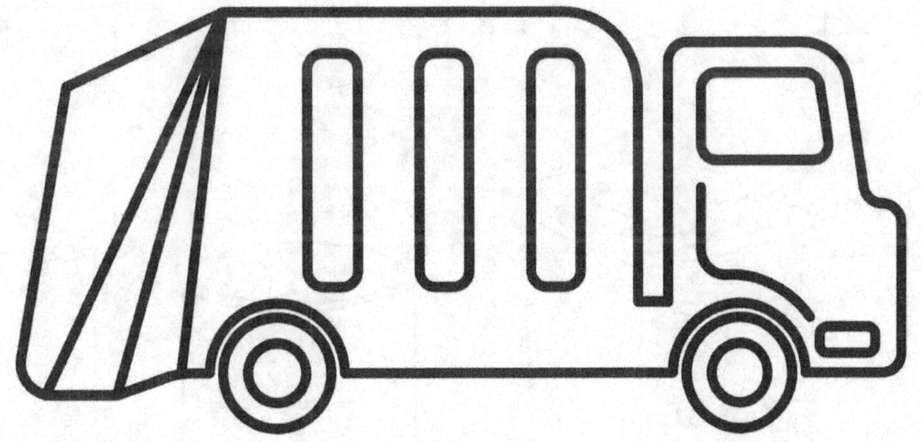

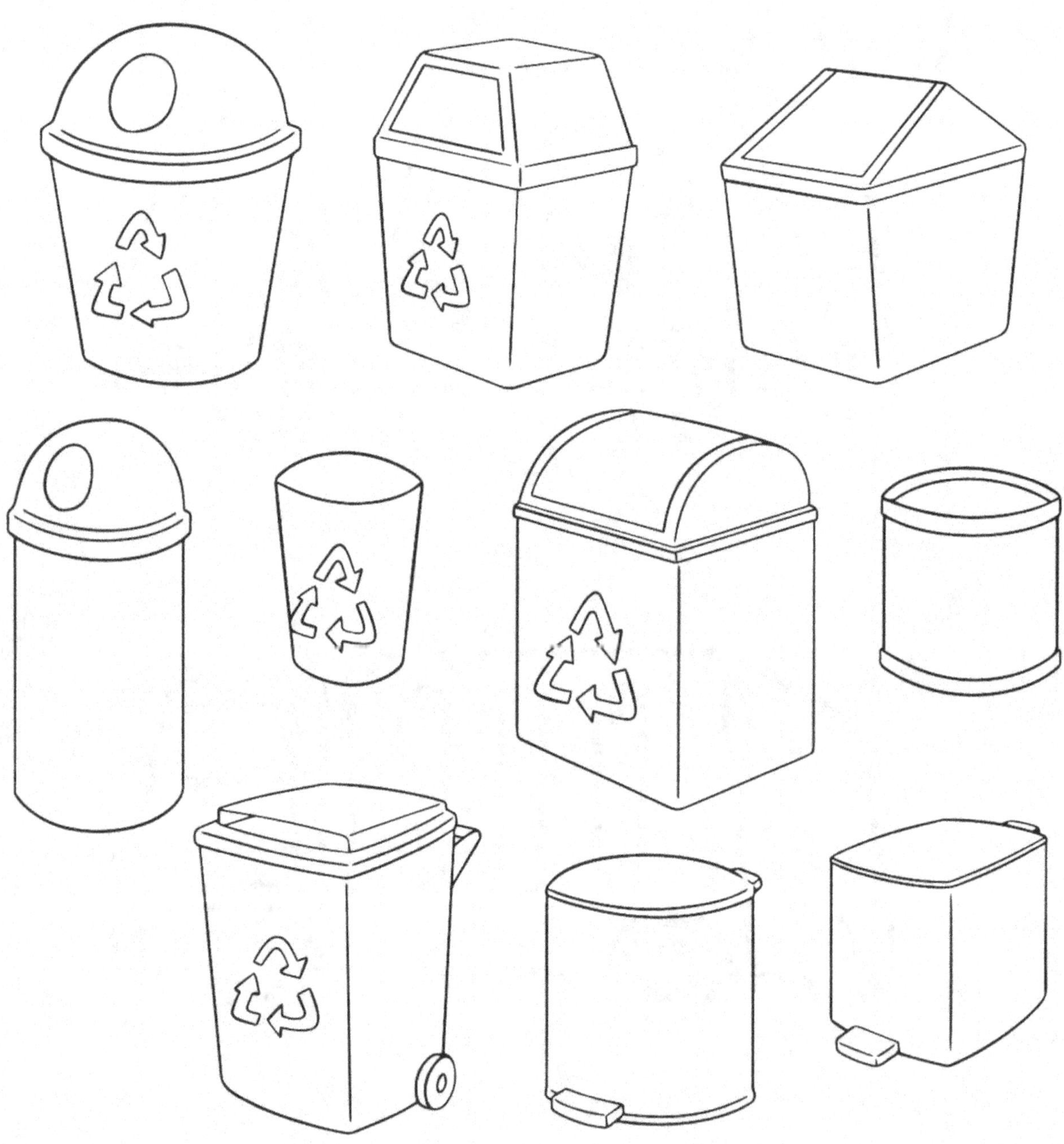

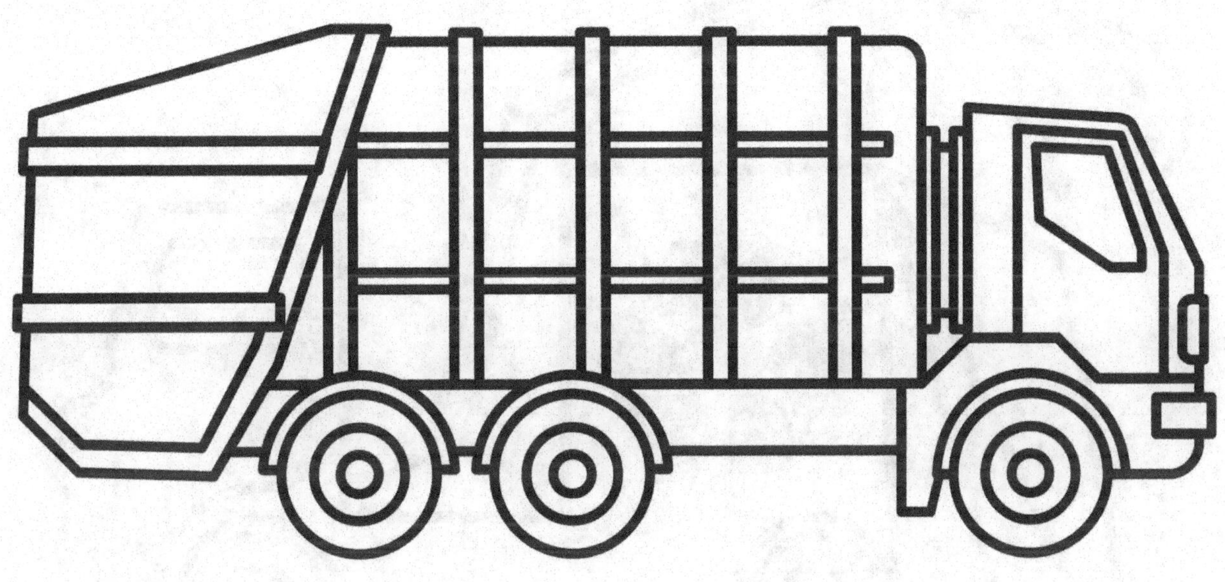

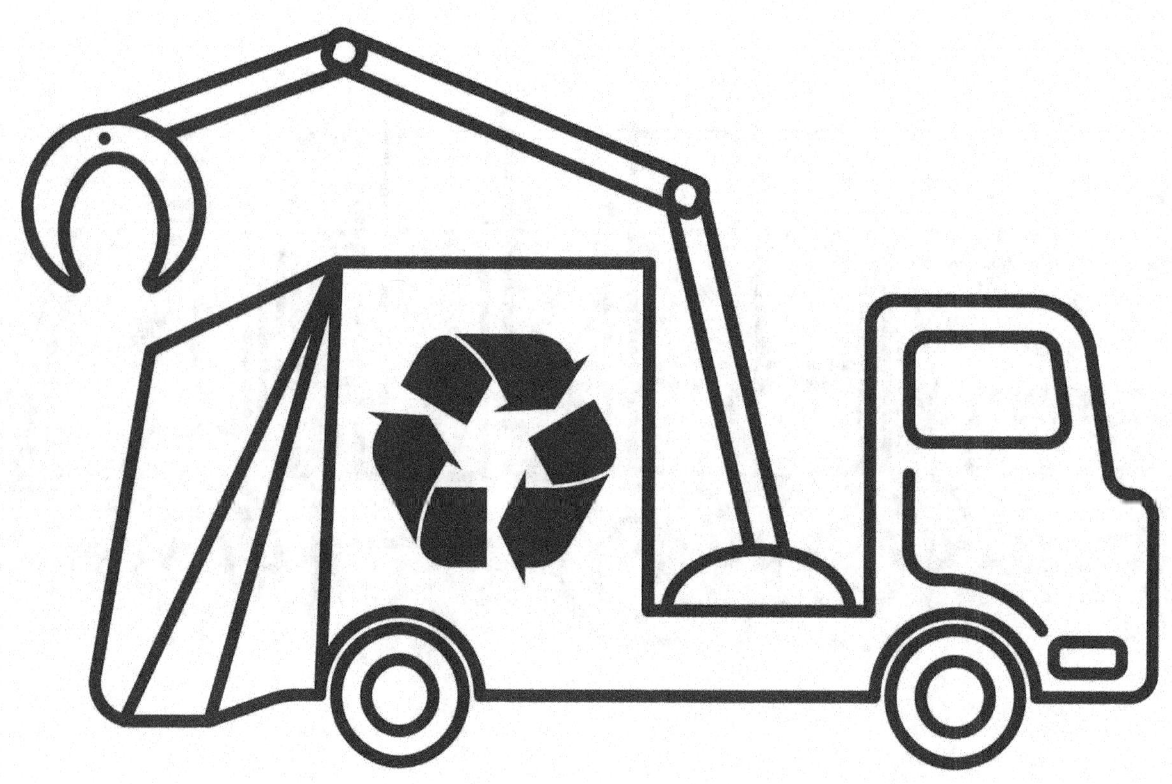

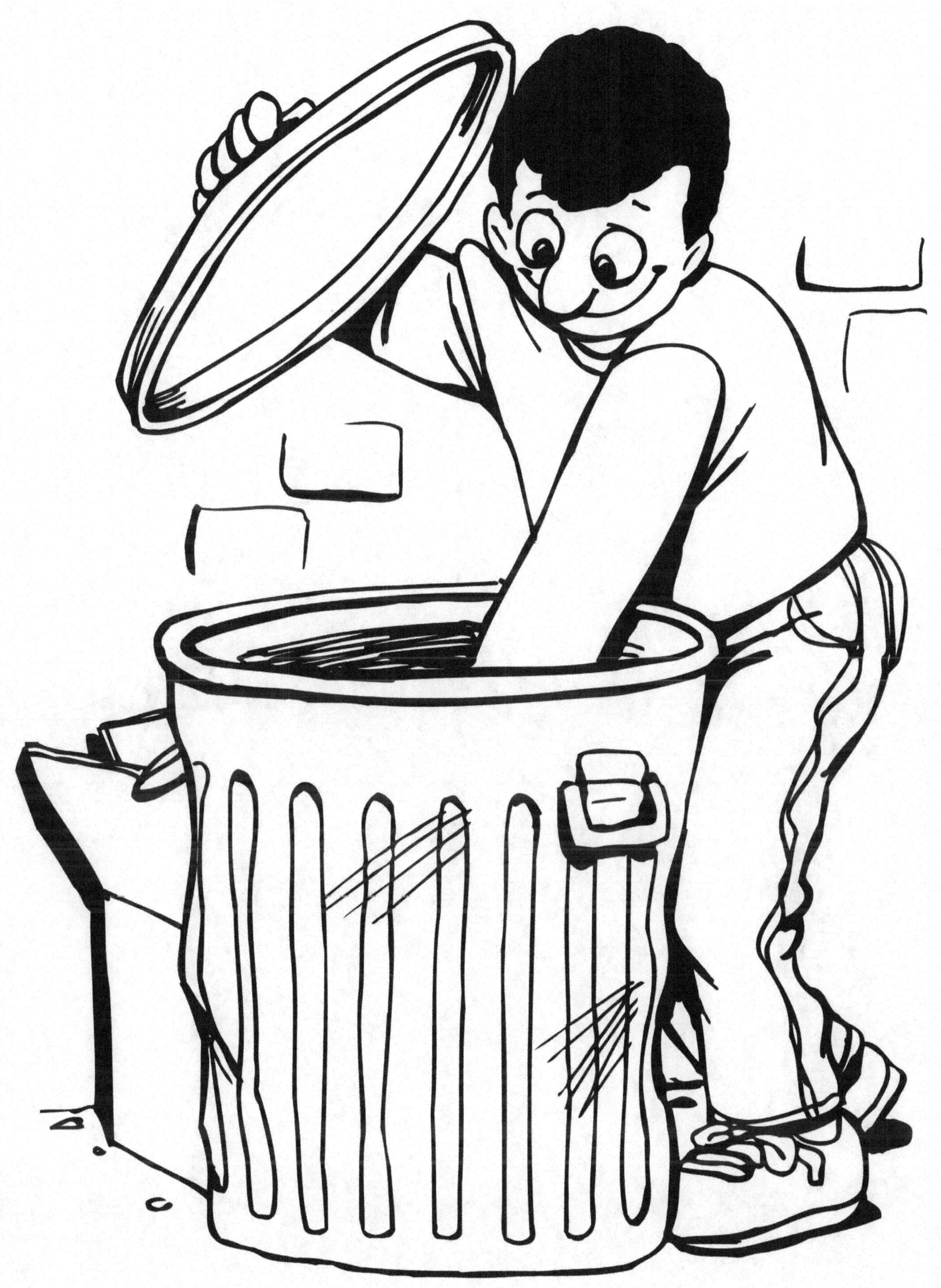

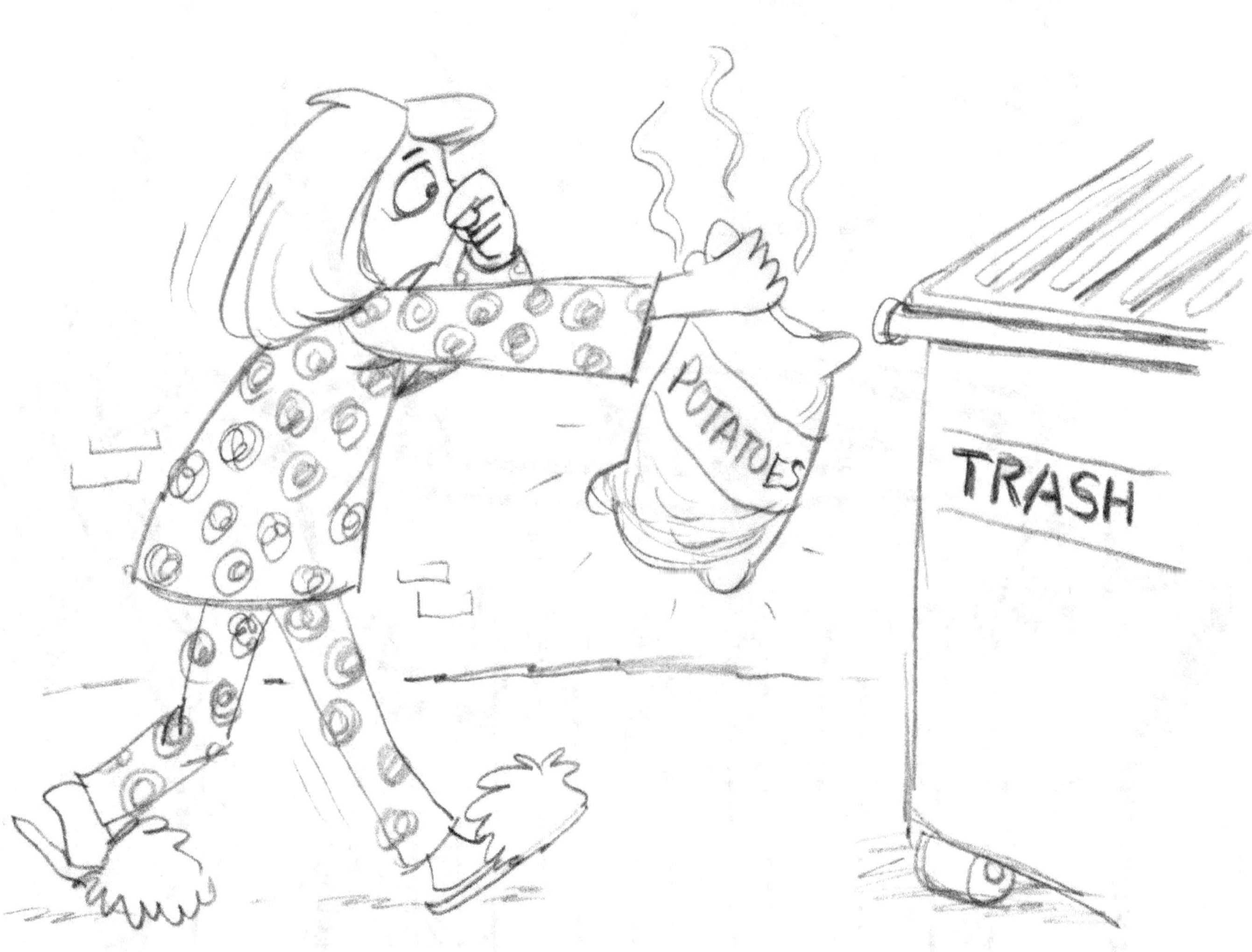

POTATOES
TRASH